Making Money with your art and designs on Redbubble

By E.C.Cook

Introduction

This book is for artists and designers who want to work from home for themselves making money from their own work. It's for the beginner in the print on demand world from someone who's been doing this for some time.

I've been designing and putting my art on products online since 2002. Many print on demand sites have popped up in that time. One of the more recent and successful ones is RedBubble.com I joined Redbubble in 2011 and since then have added all of my art and designs and am making around a thousand dollars a month on their platform. This combined with etsy and other sites gives me enough to live on and support my family of four. It is all possible! This book focuses on RedBubble.com because I find it to be the easiest to learn and use as a beginner to the print on demand marketplace.

Here is my income on redbubble from the past 6 months:

The 4th quarter of the year is always the best time as everyone is buying gifts for their loved ones for Christmas. Not every artist has to be a starving artist and I am proof of that. All it takes is a bit of know-how and effort and you can make a bit of money from your art and design work. How much you make on redbubble will be determined by your own efforts and art. You've taken the first step in getting this book — educating yourself is the key to hitting the ground running.

In the first half of the book I'll do a basic walkthrough of what you need to know and do when signing up, and the basics of uploading designs to redbubble. The second half of the book I will discuss different ways of promoting your work and the keys to being successful long term on the redbubble platform. I hope by the end of this book you will feel confident in putting your designs on various products and promoting your work online and off. As with all things making money on redbubble does take time, but with effort you can make money on redbubble.

Start with small goals and work your way up. My first goal when selling products online was to make just enough to pay a utility bill, I reached that within a few months then moved my goal up to paying rent. Now my goal is to buy a house within 5 years using money from my art and design work. As I said I have been doing this for over a decade now, so it does take time but it is very much worth your time.

Getting Started with Redbubble

SIGN UP

The first step is signing up to redbubble. Sign up is free and easy. You'll want to pick your brand name, whether that is your real name or not is up to you. You may want to pick a name that you can also create a facebook fanpage using and a pinterest board. Make sure to google the name you want to use to make sure it isn't already being used by someone else. Not only so as not to step on their toes but to keep your branding unique.

You should take a few days to think of the name you want to use. Google it, investigate it and see if you can buy the domain name. If you aren't already using other platforms like pinterest and Instagram you'll want to sign up to those with the same name if at all possible.

Some technical and legal things to consider when siging up – some of this info seems common knowledge. But I feel the need to share – from redbubble:

Members must be 16 years or older. This is a legal requirement as people under the age of 16 are not able to enter into a legal contract with Redbubble. Sorry to those who are younger. In the meantime keep on creating and planning for your 16th birthday!

On Mature content - *Mature Content refers to works containing content that may be considered not suitable for viewing by some audiences, such as nudity, blood, guns, alcohol, drugs, violence, adult language and other similar themes.*

Artists and designers should indicate that their work is Mature Content as a part of the upload process; however this can also be done at any time using the

Edit Work function.

IF your work is more mature, please don't offer it on children's clothing, this is in bad taste and could get you banned from redbubble!

More on what Redbubbble has to say about nudity and pornography:

The following material is not permissible on Redbubble:

- *Sexual material: Explicit and gratuitous foreplay. Displays of sexual intercourse showing genitalia in direct contact including, but not limited to, male-to-*

female, female-to-female and male-to-male. Male or female masturbation where hands come into contact with genitalia in real or simulated masturbation/fondling. Semen and vaginal fluids. Urine when considered in a sexual context. "Sex toys" in use with genitalia or in a clear sexual context including but not limited to penis-rings, dildos, strap-ons, vibrators etc. Manually spread vaginas or anuses (either sex) by hand or manipulated open by any other artificial means.

- Penises and vaginas: Any image that is deemed to be gratuitous - definition of gratuitous: "unnecessary or unwarranted". This will generally include close-up vagina images or images that show intimate details of a vagina, men with an erection that is clearly visible, or images where the penis is the focal subject.

- Nude or 'sexualized' children: Redbubble has a conservative approach to images of children. Children should be appropriately clothed. As a general rule, 'appropriately clothed' means no genitalia, no uncovered bottoms and, for pubescent girls, no bare chests. We define a child as anyone under the age of 18. In images of babies or infants, some nudity is acceptable (for example, in the style of Anne Geddes' portrait photography) but we request that genitalia is covered.

General titillation: Images constructed with the primary purpose of sexually exciting the viewer and where no attempt at an artistic statement has been made.

...and violence:

Work that glorifies or trivializes violence is not permitted. This includes graphic depictions of violence, works that trivialize violent acts, and work or behavior where the intent of the artist is to incite hatred or violence.

Works that deal with catastrophic events such as genocides or holocausts need to be sensitively handled. Works that have the potential to cause the victims serious distress may be removed.

...and racism: *Racist content or behavior and material designed to incite racism is not permitted. We define racism as either the hatred or intolerance of another race, or a belief that all members of a* racial group possess characteristics specific to that race, especially to distinguish it as being inferior.

Racist Terms: Works that use racist terms in a casual and/or derogatory way are not permitted. The decision to remove a work will depend on the context in which words are used, but as a rule of thumb this excludes situations where legitimate discussion or commentary is taking place. For example, a written work where the artist uses the word 'nigger' in the context of describing her personal experiences of racism would be allowed to remain, but a slogan t-shirt featuring the word would not.

Use of symbols: Symbols and icons carry strong messages e.g. the swastika, crosses, and the Koran. These symbols and their like can be used in a work, but only with considerable care. If the intent is ambiguous, needlessly provocative or appears deliberately designed to contravene anti-vilification, anti-racist or hate guidelines then the work may be removed.

Before getting into the print on demand world you will want to educate yourself on a bit of copyright law. Basically, you cannot legally profit from someone else's work name, etc. If your art is all fanart or drawings of celebrities, you cannot put it on redbubble and profit from it unless you have expressed written permission form the copyright owner.

As redbubble puts it:

Copyright and other forms of IP protection

Redbubble respects Copyright and Trademark laws and will remove any work found to infringe Copyright or Trademark protection. If you believe your copyright or other intellectual property rights are being infringed, you are able to make a formal complaint by using the processes described in our policy."

Best case scenario if you are violating copyright or trademark laws is that redbubble bans your account, worst case is you get sued by the copyright owners, so really, just don't do it sort term gain is not worth the very real and long term risk.

TAXES

I am not a lawyer, or an accountant, and this advice is just advice from one artist to another and this is based on USA taxes - – save at least 30% of your earnings on redbubble for taxes. You will need to fill out a tax form with your SS# and you will get a form at the beginning of the year from redbubble for filing your taxes. I only want you to be prepared for this because unlike employers redbubble does not take any taxes out of your earnings, you are an generally seen as an independent contractor – sole proprietor and as commissions they are taxed as a business meaning you will pay 100% of your social security and Medicaid AND your taxes, if you are making lots of money on redbubble and are worried about such things you may want to invest some of your earnings into talking with a tax lawyer or accountant.

Once you've created your account you'll want to check out....

PRODUCT PRICING

Under account details you can set your product pricing; you'll want to do this before you start to upload. Too many artists undervalue their work here. If you price cheaply customers will see your products as cheap. I general keep my markups above 25% on all print on demand sites that let you set your own markup. For some of the more expensive products like leggings I'll go as low as 16%, but I need to be making at least $5.00 on most products, stickers being the exception. My Markup on stickers is 80% and I sell many stickers every day on RB.

Where you set your prices is up to you. But again, don't sell yourself short. You can make $5.00 for every shirt sold or 2$, but remember at 2$ a shirt you will need to sell more than double the shirts to make the same amount that I do at 5$ a shirt. Thankfully as of right now redbubble lets you play with and change prices at any time, so try different price points and see what works best for you and your brand.

GETTING PAID

Payment cycles begin at the start of each month and are usually processed by the 7th of the month. Redbubble pays via paypal, bank transfers, or checks, so you'll want to set those up right away to make sure you don't miss a payment. The checks take a little longer as they are coming "snail mail".

Payment thresholds depend on the payment method

and currency in the US for paypal it is only $20.00, so once you make 20, you will receive payment the next month.

PROFILE

Once you've created an account you'll want to create a profile as well. Your profile should tell buyers a bit about yourself and your inspirations. Tell them your story, what mediums you use and what sorts of things they can expect from your shop. You can easily link to your facebook page, instagram and other social media platforms from your page, which you will want to do. The more your links and name are out there the better for your business. Never pass up an opportunity to link to one of your pages and describe your art. Getting followers on all platforms is very powerful stuff; I'll discuss this more later on in the book.

You want to make sure you have the box checked to

receive "Bubblemail" This is the only way for a buyer or penitential buyer to contact you through redbubble. I've gotten many bubblemails thanking me for my art, with compliments but more importantly I've gotten lots of opportunities from other companies and people who want something personalized by having a place for a buyer to easily message me.

UPLOADING

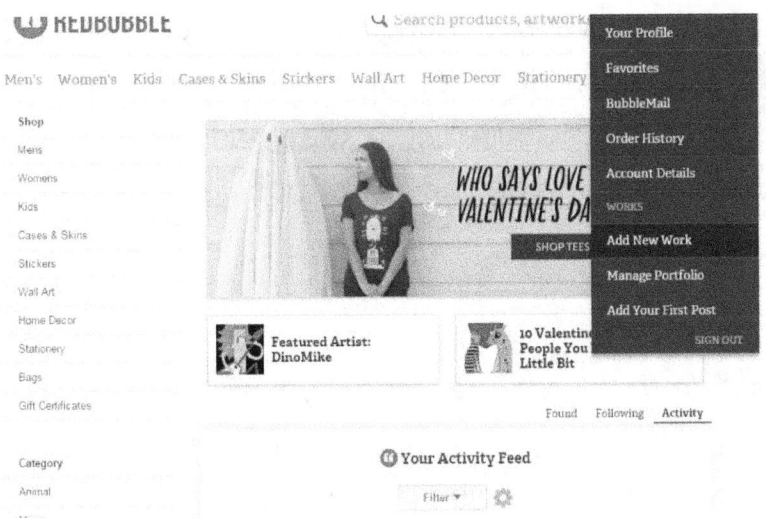

Once you've opened your account and created a profile linking to your other sites you'll want to start uploading as soon as possible. The only way to get good at and quick at uploading is really through trial and error. Redbubble has a very user friendly "what you see if what you get" uploader. As with any website the file you use will need to be big generally 300 DPI, this makes for clean nice looking prints. Redbubble accepts PNG files and JPG, I recommend PNG as most websites require PNG.

Here, from the website listing (as of January 2016) are the recommended sizes for each product they currently offer It's a nice list to keep hady when you are just starting the design for redbubble–

*"Take note that larger sized designs will be scaled down to fit the smaller dimensions, whereas smaller designs will **not** be scaled up. As this handy video explains, our uploader will stop a design from being added to certain products if it doesn't meet their minimum requirements. If you'd like to use a*

single image file for every product, we'd recommend starting with at 13500×11462 pixels (suitable for our king size duvet covers). That way it'll be big enough to fit every product we offer!

Greeting Cards:

1300x900 pixels (1 megapixel) more info on cropping, borders and aspect ratio for cards here(link to Aspect ratios for greeting cards)

Framed Prints and Stretched Canvas:

2400×1600 pixels (4 megapixels) for the small print

3240×2160 pixels (7 megapixels) for the medium print

3840×2560 pixels (10 megapixels) for the large print

Metal Prints:

Extra Small - 2400 x 2400 pixels

Small - 3200 x 3200 pixels

Medium - 3600 x 3600 pixels

Large - 3840 x 3840 pixels

Extra Large - 4800 x 4800 pixels

Posters:

2500×3500 pixels for the smallest print

3500×5000 pixels for the medium print

5000×7100 pixels for the large print

Calendar images:

2182x1906 pixels for the months

2371x2875 pixels for the cover

Art Prints:

3840x3840 pixels will cover all sizes up to extra large. Art Prints dimensions can change, floating your different shaped images whilst the paper sizes remain the same. More details on Art Print paper sizes is available on the product page.

Apparel:

2400×3200 pixels will cover the printable area, although you can resize larger images to fit when uploading. The file must be a PNG for transparencies to be saved.

Mens Graphic tee

3873x4814 pixels will cover the printable area. There is further information on graphic tees including an artist's template available over here.

Stickers:

600x800 pixels for small size

1100x1100 pixels for medium size

1700x1700 pixels for large size

2800x2800 pixels for X-Large size

The file must be a PNG for transparencies to be saved. We recommend uploading a file with the maximum pixel requirements (2800 x 2800px) to ensure your design is available on all 4 sticker sizes

Phone Cases & Skins:

1187x1852 pixels will cover the printable area, however you can resize larger images to fit

Laptop Skins & Studio Pouches:

4600x3000 pixels will cover the printable area, however you can resize larger images to fit

Please note slight cropping of the image on the smaller pouches will occur

Laptop Sleeves:

4125px x 2956px for all sizes.

iPad Cases & Skins:

2696 x 3305 pixels will cover the printable area

Throw Pillows:

2188x2188 pixels for the small pillow

2438x2438 pixels for the medium pillow

2788x2788 pixels for the large pillow

Tote Bags:

2175x2175 pixels for the small tote bag

2625x2625 pixels for the medium tote bag

2950x2950 pixels for the large tote bag

Drawstring Bags:

2475x2775 pixels for drawstring bags

Duvet Covers (125 max DPI):

8570x11250 pixels for the twin duvet (including bleeding)

11000x11000 pixels for the queen duvet (including bleeding)

13500×11462 pixels for the king duvet (including bleeding)

Mugs:

2700x1624 pixels for standard & tall mug

2376x2024 pixels for travel mug

Leggings:

4350x4032 pixels for leggings.

Scarves:

5748x5748 pixels for scarves.

Pencil Skirt:

2152x2502 pixels for pencil skirts.

Drawstring Bag:

2475x2775 pixels for drawstring bags.

Spiral Notebooks:

1756x2481 pixels for spiral notebooks.

Hardcover Journals:

3502x2385 pixels for hardcover journals.

Color

We recommend using the sRGB colour profile to get your works looking as glorious as possible. Some products, such as t-shirts will print in the CMYK colour spectrum, but we can safely say that this conversion will happen automatically during printing."

As you can see, redbubble offers many products at this point and the list is growing. My personal recommendation is to use one template for all products. I use a 15x18 inch 300 DPI RGB template with a transparent background in photoshop for all of my files. I go big because as redbubble says they will make it smaller for smaller products, but they cannot make it bigger. This is what my personal template looks like in photoshop:

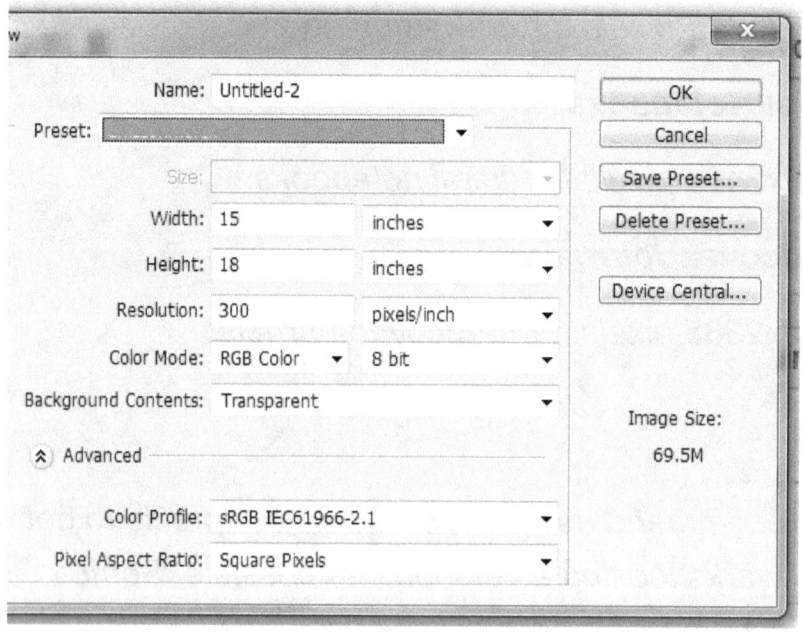

If you need help understanding file types and how to create a template in photoshop or in your photo software please know that youtube is your friend with the basics of files and designing. I recommend searching youtube for videos on anything you do not understand as there are many great and free how-to videos. Again the key to success is education don't let not understanding something be a roadblock for you.

Because Redbubble has a "what you see is what you get" uploader you can easily adjust your images on the products themselves once you've uploaded. Go ahead and try an image file in their design tool to get used to it and how it works. Trial and error is great for understanding how it works. You can always delete the products later very easily or not go through the whole process at once.

While your file is uploading, you can fill in all the details about your work like the relevant tags, available products for sale and the artist markup. You also have the ability to pick the title for your work and add in other important details.

You will want to use every keyword you can think of here without being irrelevant because this is how google and Redbubble "see" your work. Describe the subject and colors. Are there any holidays that your art would fit in with? As in, if it were a drawing of an evergreen I would definitely use the tag Christmas in there, and if it were a drawing of a cake I would use the word birthday. Don't use irrelevant tags; you don't want customers to see something they weren't at all searching for and this could potentially get you in trouble with redbubble. This is exactly what redbuble has to say about tags and tag spamming:

Tag Spamming

Tag spamming is not permitted. Tag spamming is the use of irrelevant or inappropriate words in the tags on a work - for example, using the tag blue on a work that contains only red, or using adult themed tag words on children's clothing or works that reference children."

For each product type, you can do some basic editing before saving the work for final upload.

From Redbubble's website:

1. *In case you ever lose your design file, you can always come back and download it here.*
2. *If you have a file specifically for tees, you can upload it here.*
3. *Use this drop down menu to select which style of tee you wish to appear for the preview.*
4. *Choose if you would prefer the design to default to the front or back of the garment.*
5. *Pick a default colour, and customize the colour range available for your design here.*

6. *Reduce the size of your design by using this scale slider.*
7. *Play with the centre design feature, either vertically or horizontally.*
8. *Change the mark up percentage and product availability here.*
9. *Re-position your design by clicking and dragging this preview*

The nice part is the slider. You can make your image bigger (no bigger than the original file, of course) or smaller depending on the product or even tile your image. It is in my opinion the best print on demand marketplace uploader out there so far and others could really learn a lot from them.

YOUR ART/DESIGNS

Of course not all art works on all products. Most work on prints and stickers, some are great for leggings and shirts. The best-selling items by far are the shirts on Redbubble, and if you want to make good money you'll want to sell more than just stickers at Redbubble.

If you are good with image editing programs like illustrator or Photoshop you'll want to "take out the backgrounds" where you are able to with artwork so they'll look good on shirts. Because redbubble lets you change the file for different products you can take the time to use different files that fit the product better if you are able.

For instance, much of my art has backgrounds which are great for prints, tote bags and laptops skins but it doesn't at all work for shirts. So I go into photoshop and basically remove the background just leaving the subject of the art for a shirt design. Of course you may need to learn some basic photoshop skill to do this but it is very much worth it because, again, shirts are their best-selling product.

Not only should to edit your art for various products, but try adding text to your art if it works. DaFont.com has many "free for commercial use" fonts you can use in conjunction with your art to create wonderful and unique shirts that no one else has. Have a nice bass fish painting? Add "I Love Fishing" text to it and you have a completely separate design to sell with the same art. The possibilities are endless and adding text to art gives you that many more designs to sell on the platform.

Once you have set up your profile and uploaded at least 5 different artworks or designs you can move onto –

PROMOTING YOUR WORK

Redbubble makes lots of this easy; one thing that is easily missed and has brought me many repeat buyers is the "buyer's message". In your account click on "promote" and you should see this:

Message to your buyers

SAVE MESSAGE

It's a handy place to write a thank you message to buyers. This is a great opportunity to drive customers to your other sites. OR you could ask them to take a picture of their product with a specific hashtag on Instagram or twitter so you can search for it and thank them. I go back and forth from having it say something like "Thank you for your purchase, check out our site at www.myblog.com" to "Thanks for your purchase! Share your product images with the #showme on Instagram!" Both work well in keeping buyers connected and if/when you see someone share your product on Instagram be sure to thank them!

Outside of Redbubble and its tools there are a millions ways to promote your stuff, okay, maybe not millions but lots and lots. It all depends on your specific niche and what you enjoy doing. One thing is for sure though – you need to be on multiple social media platforms and use them daily. Not all for promotion either – you want to engage your audience, not just sell to them. No one wants to follow an Instagram that is all shirts all the time. People don't want ads, they want engaged.

Let's say all of your art is breastfeeding art, or parenting related, kids and family stuff. You'd want to post a lot about parenting, breastfeeding and family. Follow other blogs and Instagram pages related to those things and comment often. Participate in the community you want to eventually sell to. This is where passion comes in. If you don't care about the niche you are selling you won't have much success here. You need to be involved.

So here's the sites that I recommend you sign up to

right away if you have not already and a little bit about them:

Make **a facebook Fanpage or group.** This depends on what you're doing. You may want both. A fanpage is great if you are an artist, a group is great to create a community based on a niche (like breastfeeding) everyone is on facebook from 13-101, so you can reach any target demographic this way. If you want to get some follows on a fan page or people to join your group you can always run a cheap ad directed at the people who love your niche for about $5.00 to start off. Once you get going and people share posts it gets easier to get fans and members.

Instagram is an all ages platform for picture sharing, use hashtags to find other interested in the same subjects Post photos daily and use 5 hashtags per post (not too many, never to few)

Pinterest mainly women over the age of 25, family

oriented, weddings, etc, but with hashtags and a bit of searching you can find anything. It may not be the best place to find, say, fishermen though. Be sure to describe your "pins"

WaNeLo which stands for want/need/love very similar to pinterest but with a younger more "hip" audience. This is great for those who have a younger teen audience.

Twitter All ages, again use hashtags to find your audience. Engage! Add pictures to your tweets to make them more interesting, or you can connect your instagrams to twitter and share those pictures on both – multitask where you can!

Tumblr a younger demographic, use tags to find the audience and share interest. It's easy to see how big your audience is there by simply signing up and doing a few tag searches, see how many people are posting about your particular niche.

With all of these platforms you will want to start by following people who have a similar interest and comment on their posts, but not until you've make a few posts yourself so they have something to see when checking your page out.

You may not have time for all of those, but you'll want to at least sign up. From there pick two or three that you are going to spend some time with daily. I use Instagram, facebook, tumblr and pinterest a whole lot because that's where I have the most fun and have found my audience. You want to use the ones you find easy to navigate and have fun with for yourself. You don't want it to be a chore, that's why you want to use the ones you find the most fun.

If you use your phone a whole lot you may find Instagram and twitter work best. If you're using a desktop the most pinterest and tumblr might be better, though they all work on both mediums some are just better as apps.

Redbubble makes it easy to share your products form the product page they have links to many social media sites including facebook, twitter, tumblr, pinterest, google+, and instragram. Use them wisely. I space mine out and it depends on the site. You can get away with sharing a bit more products on pinterest because it is mainly a shopping site – people pin the things they like. But you won't get away with that at twitter or Instagram . Again, engage the audience.

I'll use Instagram as an example. You cannot put links into the description of your photos on Instagram but you can have a link on your profile. I link to my website, which links to my redbubble, but you could also just link to your redbubble profile.

People on Instagram don't want to see a product

page, they want lovely true to life photos. So I share a whole lot of true to life pictures. I share picture of me creating art. Photos from outside, photos of me wearing my shirts, or my kids wearing my shirts. I share pictures of the prints I've purchased. YES! You will want to purchase at least a few or your products to at least see what they are like in "real life" and take a few your own good quality pictures of these products and share them on all of your platforms.

I only share pictures of my products every 5 or so pictures! You don't want to annoy people or look like an ad account on any platform. I search hashtags related to my latest picture and comment and like others pictures. I follow people who I think might like my stuff. I use 5 hashtags on all of my pictures as well as a long description to engage with my audience and so that they can find me! Engagement is the key on all of the platforms and they all have their own communities, know them, and work within them.

You can easily link your redbubble account to your

personal facebook account, and if you think your friends won't mind getting auto-updates in their feed every time you post a new design then link them, but remember your friends and family generally are not your audience and if you are posting daily you may want to rethink this, as people may get annoyed and hide you from their feed.

I think it's best to not have auto-updates and just post yourself when you feel like it to your personal Facebook. This way you can add some text, talk about the design or artwork and, again, engage your audience in conversation. Generally the only time I share my redbubble with my personal friends is when there's some great promotion going on at redbubble, then I tend to post about it everywhere. Free shipping is always a good thing, and people who normally may not buy are more likely to do so with a nice discount of some sort.

IF YOU LOVE WRITING be sure to get some sort of blog going, having your own domain is nice, but if you do not sign up to blogger for free. It's run by google and tends to do well in google search rankings, plus it is extremely easy to use and has a build in member base of blogs you can follow (and they may follow back) like other social media you'll want to update on a regular basis. Write about process in your art-making, show your work in progress, people love to see the "behind the scenes". If you want you can also share your success stories when you start making money on redbubble.

GET CONNECTED

Not only do you want to keep tabs on what's being said on Redbubble's blog (http://blog.redbubble.com/) for tips and tricks but you also want to check out the various Redbubble facebook groups run by regular members of redbubble.

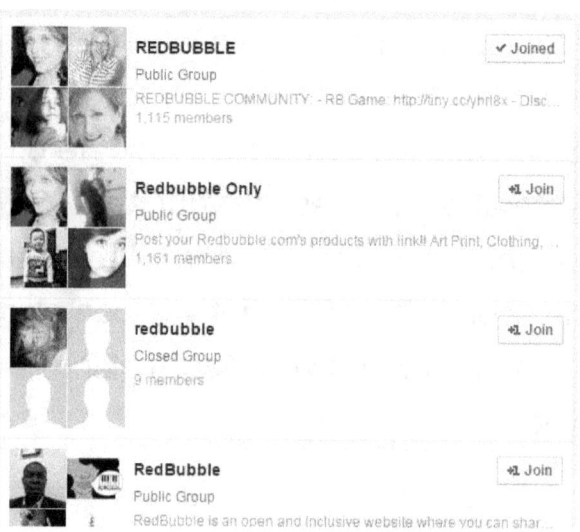

These groups are essential and are coming and going all of the time. I recommend you simple search facebook for "Redbubble" then sort by groups and at first just join them all – once you figure out which ones work for you, you can leave the rest at any time.

By being a member of these sorts of groups you will be one of the first to know of any changes or new products added to redbubble. This is how I know quickly when redbubble has added a new product so that I can be one of the first artists to design for that product. The earlier you add your art to new products the more eyeballs will see that product and that equals sales.

And finally,

ESSENTIALS TO REMEMBER:

Upload every single week. More if you can. This of course means you need to be creating new art and designs on almost a daily basis. Remember to look at your art in a different way – try to use it a few times, once without text, and then try adding text. Change it around in photosohp or illustrator to get a complex new design. The great part about this is the more you create, the better you will get at the whole process. After a year of uploading on a weekly basis you will be making money from redbubble, this I am sure of, unless you are tagging horribly! Which brings me to…

Tag and describe your work this is something I see so many people just do flat out WRONG. You need to be thinking of at least 10 good tags for each design. The color, medium, subject, any holidays that would work well with the design in mind (e.g. breastfeeding art tagged mother's day, a snowy scene tagged Christmas) Also tag the season, summer, fall, etc. You want a minimum of 10 relevant tags. Think of what people would search for if they wanted something like your art.

Participate in the community this means the redbubble community AND social media communities you've chosen as discussed earlier in the book. Participate in them every day in a meaningful way.

This Takes Time+Effort it is not a get rich quick with no talent scheme, it does take work, but with time and effort you can and will make money on redbubble. Do not expect to get paid in that first month, but do have goals. If you do everything this book suggests you should see sales within the first few months.

IN CLOSING

Don't give up easily! Work on your art and designs every day and go make your money. There is a buyer for every art style, you just have to get the products out there for them to find. No artist or designer who puts the work and effort in should be a "starving artist" you don't have to be in galleries or be famous to make money; thanks to sites like redbubble you can make money on your art!